B is for Breast Cancer

By Anita and Simon Howell
Illustrations by Sue Roche

This story is not intended to be used as medical advice; rather we hope you will find it useful in helping you discuss your diagnosis and treatments. If you do have questions, please speak to your medical team.

Copyright © 2018 by Anita and Simon Howell
All rights reserved.

ISBN 978-1-9993136-0-9

Dear Reader
  we are sorry that Breast Cancer
        has touched your lives.

Thankyou for buying this book – we really
hope that it will help families who
have a member who is undergoing
treatment for Breast Cancer.

    Our best wishes to you and
         your family on
            your Journey.

                    Anita and Simon
                        Howell.

MERRY CHRISTMAS

SEEDS

4

Jack and I had a wonderful time this morning with Grandma and Grandad. They took us to the garden centre to look at the Christmas lights and decorations. I chose a silver star and Jack chose a snowman.

Oh, let me introduce ourselves. My name is Lucy and I am ten. I live with my little brother Jack – he's five; our Daddy whose name is Douglas and our Mummy, Ruth, who looks after all of us. Mummy enjoys crafting and I love it when Mummy and I make cards together and Jack really enjoys doing junk modelling.

Mummy and Daddy came home just before teatime and we told them all about our exciting morning and showed them our new Christmas decorations.

Mummy said that she had something to tell us too. She told us that she and Daddy had seen a doctor and that the doctor had said that Mummy has **Breast Cancer**.

7

Mummy and Daddy told Jack and me that Cancer is an illness that starts when some of the cells in your body grow too fast. Those cells may grow into a lump that you might be able to feel. This is called a **Tumour**.

They also told us that Mummy didn't have breast cancer because of anything she or Daddy or Jack or I did, and that Mummy didn't catch cancer like a cold, and that we can't catch it from her.

I said that it was unfair that Mummy was ill. Mummy and Daddy agreed and said that however we felt was okay, whether we were angry, scared or sad, and that we didn't have to be brave. Then we all had a big family hug.

9

Mummy explained how the doctors are planning on making her better.

In a few weeks, she will begin going to hospital to have some special medicine called **Chemotherapy**. Chemotherapy drugs are very strong and kill the cancer cells and make the tumours that Mummy has in her breast and under her arm smaller. The doctor said that in Mummy's case, she will have to have six doses or 'cycles' of chemotherapy, one every three weeks. During the first three cycles, Mummy will have one mixture of chemotherapy drugs and during the second three cycles she will have a different chemotherapy drug.

The doctors don't know for sure, because everyone is different, but it's likely that Mummy's hair will fall out because of the drugs and she might feel a bit sick and very tired.

We told Mummy that we'd look after her.

11

A little while after Mummy has finished having chemotherapy she will have to have an **operation**. A Breast **Surgeon** will take out the lumps (a **lumpectomy**) and any **lymph nodes** that the cancer has spread to. Lymph nodes are found in your armpit, neck, chest, tummy and groin, and they are part of the **lymphatic system**, which is part of our **immune system**. Mummy's doctor told her that they work like filters and can trap cancer cells, so large ones may be taken out sometimes too.

Lymph nodes can also get swollen when our body fights an everyday infection and they usually go down when we are better, so big nodes or 'glands' are often not a big deal.

Some weeks after the operation, Mummy will need to have another treatment called **Radiotherapy**. These are special rays like x-rays used to kill any cancer cells that may still be there.

Mummy is having chemotherapy first as her tumour is growing fast. But other people may have an operation first; everyone is different.

It's going to be a long year this year, for Mummy having her treatments and for us looking after her. But it'll all be worth it to get her better. Did you know that men can get Breast Cancer too? I didn't, and it doesn't happen often.

Today is Christmas Day! The last few days have been lovely, which feels strange. Yesterday, Mummy and Daddy surprised us by taking us to an ice-skating show. It was lovely to see our favourite characters dancing on the ice rink. We forgot about Mummy's illness and just enjoyed ourselves together.

Today, we have been to church, opened presents, and eaten lots of Christmas dinner which Daddy cooked and was yummy – I love roast potatoes. We have also played with our new toys, told Christmas cracker jokes and watched television together. Grandma and Grandad were here too. It's been lovely having everyone together.

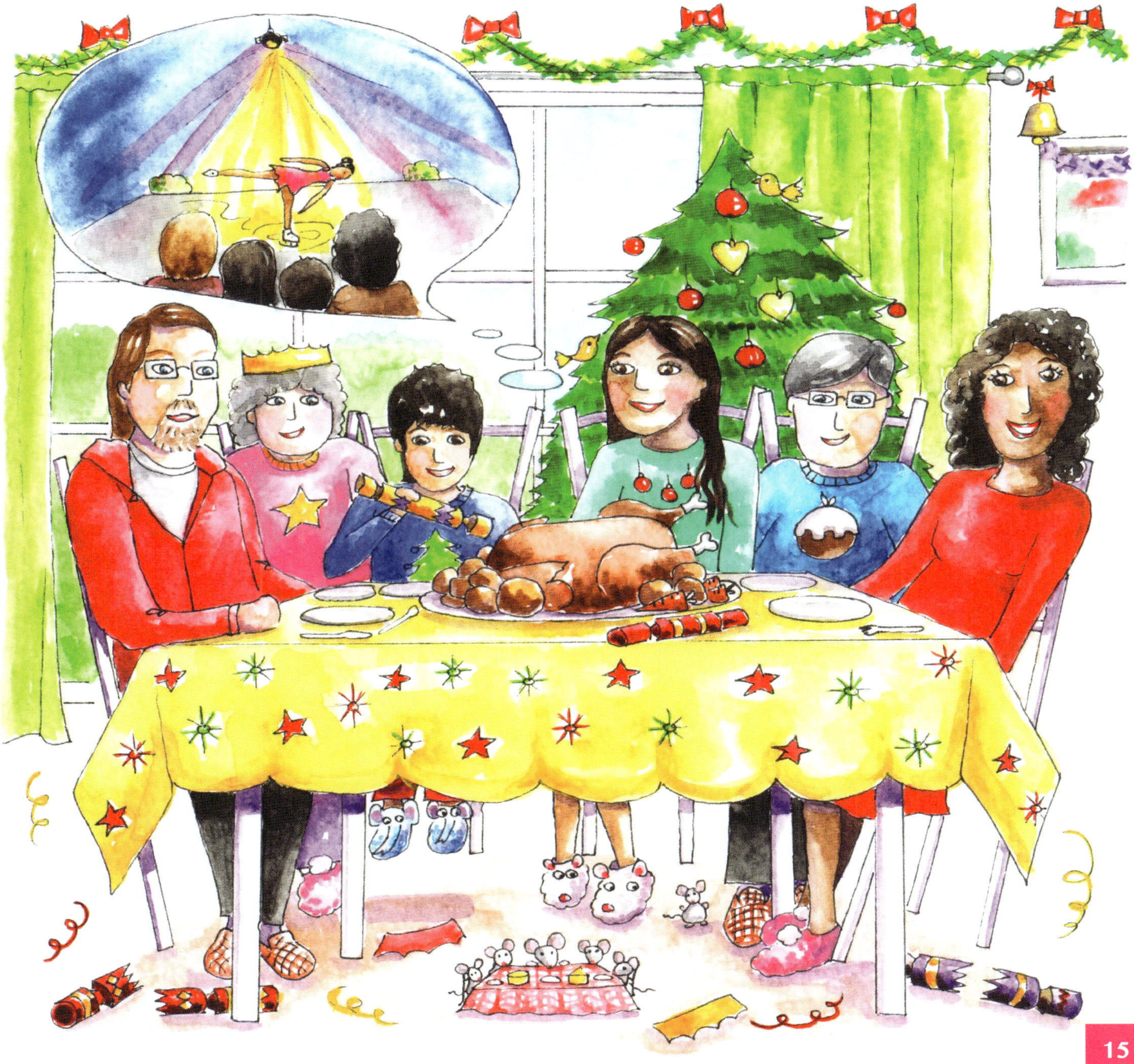

16

There are a few days left before we go back to school. Both Jack and I are looking forward to going back – it will be nice to see our friends. Mummy and Daddy will tell our teachers that Mummy is ill, so I know if I feel sad or worried at school that I will be able to talk to my teachers.

Yesterday we all went to London to a big toy shop. It was a lot of fun and we chose special cuddly toys to be Mummy-toys and Lucy-and-Jack-toys. Jack and I both chose big cuddly puppies as our Mummy-toys, and Mummy chose small puppies that she can pack in her bag when she goes to hospital as her Lucy-and-Jack-toys.

It's February and yesterday was my birthday. I am eleven now and my friends and I had a sewing party. I saw something there that I might ask Daddy to help me make for Mummy as a surprise!

Mummy has had two cycles of chemotherapy now and has felt extremely tired and says that nothing tastes good. Poor Mummy – imagine chocolate not tasting good!

She has also had to go to **A&E** a few times because she keeps getting high temperatures. The chemotherapy is weakening her immune system, so her body can't fight off infections very well. So, she must go to hospital to be given **IV antibiotics**. Antibiotics are a type of medicine used to treat bacterial infections; they can be taken as tablets or given intravenously directly into a person's vein to treat the infection quickly. To do this a nurse puts a special thin tube called a **Cannula** into a vein in Mummy's arm which is connected to the liquid antibiotics.

Sometimes Mummy is home the next day but sometimes she has had to stay in hospital for a few days. Jack and I get sad and worried when this happens, so we hug our Mummy-toys. We also write cards and draw pictures for Mummy.

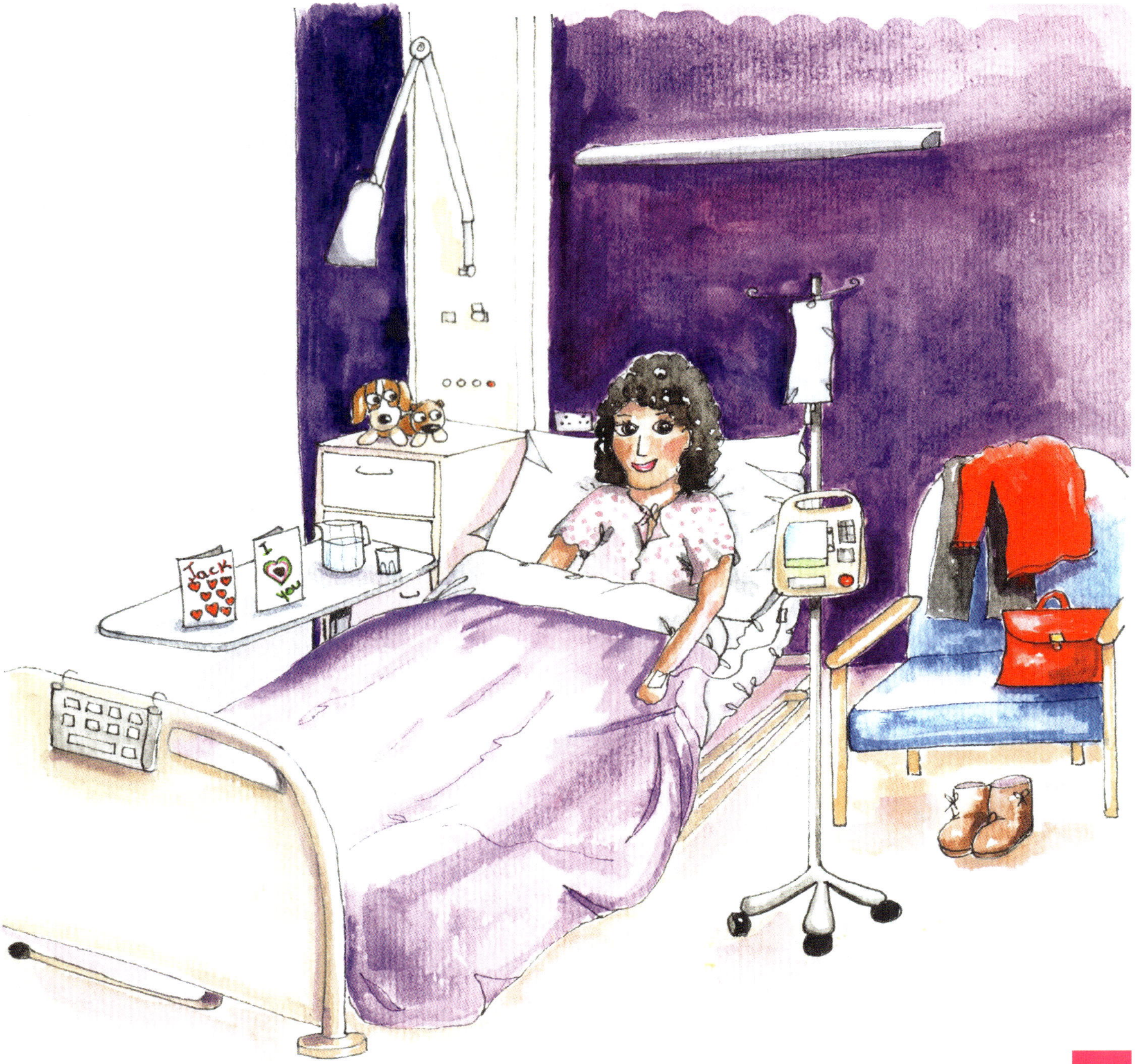
Jack
I you

20

Mummy was warned about the side effects of chemotherapy, such as sickness, tiredness, hair loss and risk of infection. But not everyone gets all the side effects. One of the things I find difficult is that Mummy's hair is falling out. In fact, last week she had it all shaved off. Jack said he thought she looked weird when we first saw her with no hair. Mummy said that was okay and that it does feel a bit strange, but we'll all get used to it.

I just want Mummy's hair to grow back soon. She says that when her hair does grow back that she hopes it will be thicker and stronger than ever.

She does have a couple of lovely wigs and a couple of caps that she wears. We had fun helping her choose them. Daddy and I even tried her wigs on which made Mummy and Jack laugh.

Whilst Mummy is going through chemotherapy, some of our friends' mums take us to and from school. Mummy says this is very helpful, as she's really tired and a bit sick. Daddy is tired too and a bit grumpy sometimes. It's hard for everyone seeing Mummy feeling ill, but it means that the medicine is working.

I want to help all I can. Mummy has discovered she can enjoy Lemon and Ginger Tea, so I have learnt to make it for her.

It's June now and Mummy finished all her chemotherapy a few weeks ago and is having her operation tomorrow. The doctors are pleased with the way that the chemotherapy worked, that the lymph nodes in Mummy's armpit are much much smaller. Mummy is going to have a lumpectomy, which means the surgeon will remove just the lump, rather than a **mastectomy** in which the surgeon removes much more of the breast.

I gave Mummy the gift that Daddy and I made. It's a heart-shaped cushion like the ones I saw at my sewing party that I had for my birthday. The lady that ran the party said that she makes these cushions and gives them to the hospital; they are then given to women like my Mummy who are having operations for breast cancer to keep them comfortable after surgery.

I said to Daddy that I wanted to make Mummy's cushion with him. I chose the fabrics and designed it and we sewed it together. Mummy loved it and said how special it was.

I told Mummy that I felt a little scared about her having an operation. She said it is perfectly normal and that she's a little scared too. However, the surgeons are very clever and do a lot of these operations, so she's in safe hands.

25

26

Mummy is home from hospital now. She only had to stay one night! Grandma and Grandad collected us from school and then Daddy took me to visit Mummy. She seemed very confused just after the operation. She asked me twice if I had a good day at school. Daddy said that it was because the strong medicine, called **anaesthesia** which made Mummy sleep during the operation, was still in her body. But Mummy would be her normal self when it wore off.

I am very glad that Mummy is home.

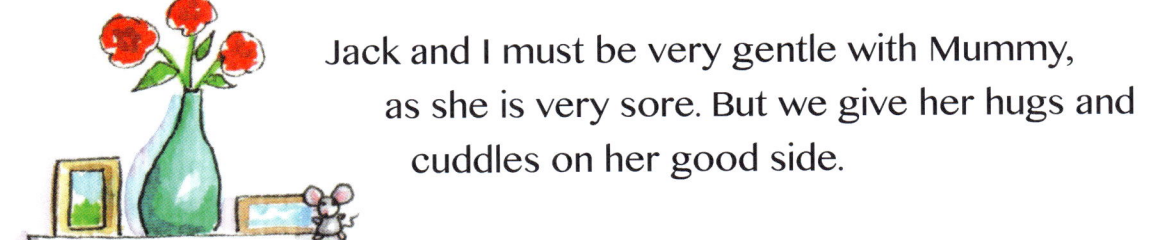

Jack and I must be very gentle with Mummy, as she is very sore. But we give her hugs and cuddles on her good side.

It's the end of August now and nearly the end of the summer holidays. We have had some lovely days out with Mummy and Daddy, including Jack's sixth birthday when we went to a castle and played in the water maze and adventure playground. We also tried archery.

My favourite day out was when we went to London. Mummy and I toured the Royal Palace, Mummy is still very sore, so we walked slowly, and she had her cushion. It was amazing, but we didn't see the Queen.

While we were doing that, Daddy and Jack went to a huge toy shop. Jack says he has had two favourite days this summer, his birthday and our day in London.

29

30

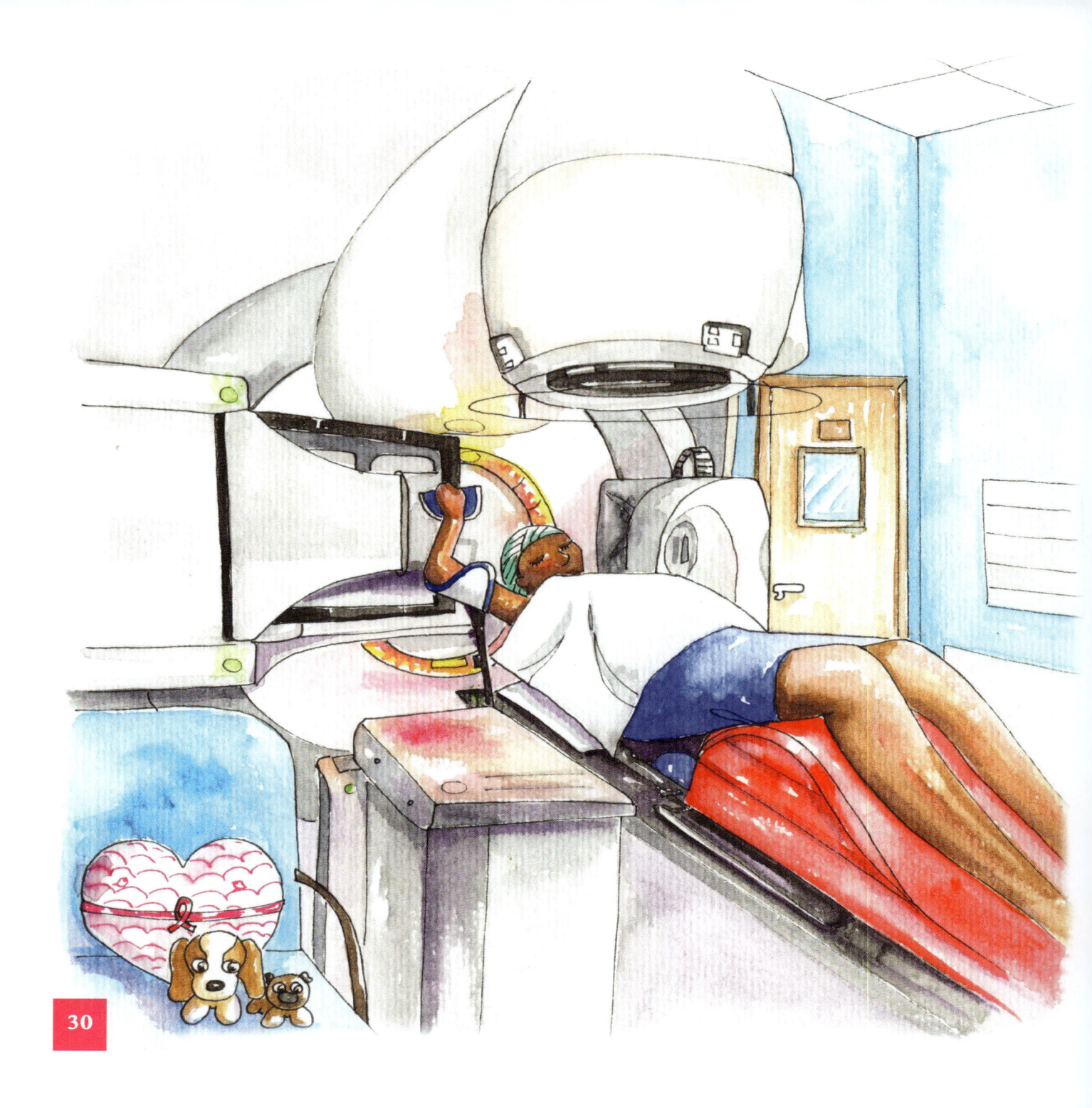

Mummy is going to start her next treatment next week, which is called Radiotherapy. Radiotherapy is a special treatment where high energy x-rays are directed at the part of the body where the tumour was. The doctors are happy that they have removed all the tumour and all the lymph nodes that had cancer. But they are still giving Mummy radiotherapy to kill any cancer cells that might be still there.

The doctors have explained that Mummy might have some side effects from the radiotherapy, such as getting very tired again and her skin might get sore. They have given her some soothing cream to help if that happens.

Mummy is going for radiotherapy daily. She has asked some friends to drive her to and from her appointments and they have set up a rota, which is very kind. It also means that Daddy can do teatime and bedtime with us as most of Mummy's appointments are in the evening.

Mummy says that she finds radiotherapy easier than chemotherapy, but she still gets extremely tired and has naps when we're at school. However, with every session, she gets nearer and nearer the end of her treatment. Jack and I are making her posters for when she has finished.

33

It's October now and nearly half term. I am looking forward to going to the **Young Carers** fun day. This is my favourite one – we do baking and craft, and I get to spend time with other children who have a parent or sibling who is ill. It's good to make friends who are also young carers. I don't like feeling alone in all this. Next year Jack will be old enough to come to the fun days too. I'm sure he will enjoy them too.

While I was at the fun day, Mummy went to the **Macmillan centre**. Macmillan are one of the cancer charities who provide lots of information and support to people who are having treatment for cancer. Mummy says it's useful to talk to other women who are going through treatment too. There are lots of complementary therapies at the centre like **counselling**, **aromatherapy** and **massage**. Mummy really likes having a massage; she says it's really relaxing.

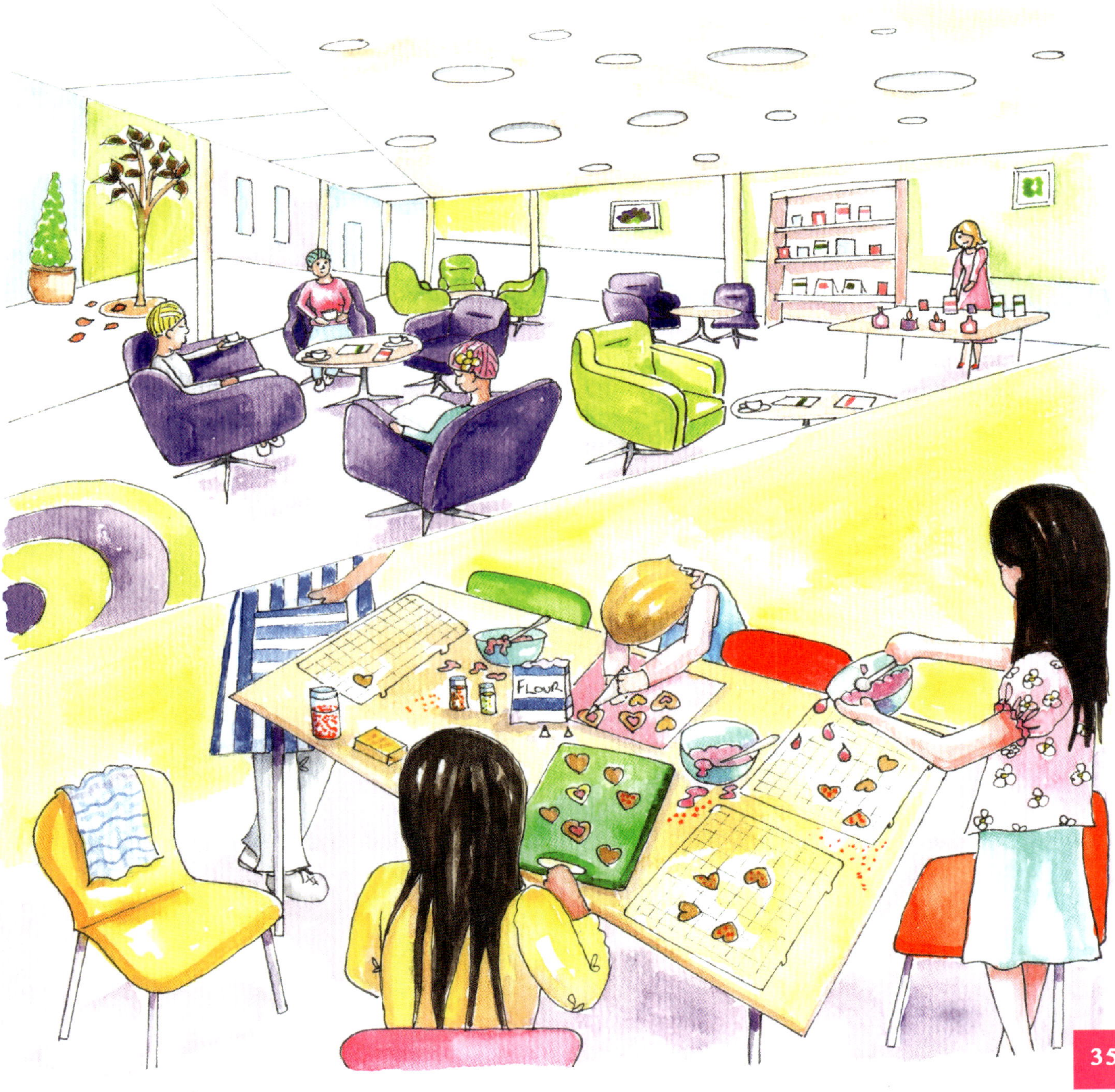
FLOUR

It's Christmas Eve today. I can't believe it's been a whole year. Jack and I had such a lovely day with Mummy and Daddy. We all went to the ice skating show again. I think we all enjoyed it so much more than last year. Last year we had only just found out that Mummy was ill. But this year she has finished all her big treatments.

She does have to take **Hormone Therapy**. This is a daily tablet and, although she gets some side effects like feeling very hot suddenly or having aches and pains in her joints and getting tearful sometimes, they are not as bad as some side effects from the other treatments. It helps prevent another tumour from starting.

37

It's Christmas day again and Jack and I are really excited! It will be lovely to celebrate Christmas and make good memories with Mummy and Daddy, and Grandma and Grandad.

I really hope that next year is a good year and we continue to make lots of fun memories as a family. This year has been very difficult at times, but Mummy says it has made her appreciate all the good things in life, especially her family and friends.

Mummy and Daddy want to have a party next year to celebrate that Mummy has finished her big treatments. It's good to see Mummy and Daddy happy and excited about the future.

39

Useful words

These are some of the more medical words we have used in this book. Knowing these words will give you and your children more control and understanding about the situation and help you talk with your doctors.

A&E Accident and Emergency, a department in a hospital for people who have been injured or are suddenly very ill.

Anaesthesia Medicine given to stop you feeling pain. Given to people before operations to make them unconscious during the operation.

Aromatherapy Use of plant extracts and essential oils. Can be used during massage.

Breast Cancer When abnormal cells in the breast grow too quickly and form lumps which can be harmful.

Cannula A thin tube which is put into a person's vein so that medicine can be given directly into the blood stream.

Chemotherapy Typically a very strong treatment for cancer where medicine is used to kill cancer cells, to stop them growing and spreading in the body.

Counselling Talking to a trained therapist who will listen to you and help you cope with your emotions.

Hormone Therapy A treatment where medicines are used to lower or block hormones in the body in order that the growth of cancer cells is stopped or slowed down.

Immune System The body's way of protecting itself against infections and other foreign bodies.

IV antibiotics   Medicines given directly into the blood stream to treat bacterial infections.

Lumpectomy   An operation where the tumour and a border of healthy tissue is removed.

Lymph Nodes   Small bean-shaped glands that are part of the immune system; they filter substances which travel through the lymphatic system and they contain white blood cells that help the body fight infection and disease.

Lymphatic System   Part of the body's immune system and involves a huge network of vessels and allows for movement of a fluid called lymph.

Macmillan Centre   Information and support centres where you can access booklets and other information free of charge. Some centres also have complementary therapies and support groups. The centres are run by the Macmillan cancer charity.

Massage   Rubbing / kneading tissues by hand or with the use of tools to aid relaxation or ease pain.

Mastectomy   An operation to remove all or part of the breast.

Operation   A surgical procedure to improve or restore a patient's health.

Radiotherapy   A treatment for diseases, including cancer, using x-rays.

Surgeon   A medical doctor who has specialised to perform operations.

Tumour   A swelling in a part of the body caused by abnormal growth of tissues. It is not always a cancer.

Young Carers   Children under 18 who have a family member who is ill (mentally or physically) or disabled and who help look after that person.

with special thanks to

Sarah and James –
Our own amazing Lucy and Jack – who make us both smile every day.
We are so proud of you! You're both loving, compassionate and amazing children!
We love you to the moon and back and twice around the universe.

Our friends and family –
Thank you for your love and support on our rollercoaster ride.
A special thank you to everyone who helped with the school runs and looked after
the children, to those who took Anita and Simon to hospital appointments and
A&E when needed, we couldn't have managed without you.

To everyone who has donated to the crowdfunding page –
Thank you so much! This book wouldn't have been possible without your help.
Thank you to everyone who shared on social media too.

About us

Thank you so much for reading this book. Anita was diagnosed with grade 3, locally aggressive Breast Cancer in December 2016. Simon has had end stage kidney failure for over a decade, been on haemodialysis and peritoneal dialysis in that time, and had (and unfortunately lost) one transplant. Our children have grown up with these difficulties.

Over the years, we have looked for books which could help our children understand the changes that were happening in their lives in relation to Kidney Disease. We found none, so in 2016 we wrote three children's books. Whilst Anita was undergoing her treatment we wrote this book. We hope that other children find this book helpful whether this topic affects their family or someone else they know.

If you would like to know more about this book and any of our other projects, please 'like' our Facebook page: **www.facebook.com/meetLucyandJack**

You can also follow us on Twitter **@MeetLucy_Jack** and on Instagram **@meetlucyandjack**

If you are looking for further information about Breast Cancer and support in the U.K, please visit:

Breast Cancer Care **www.breastcancercare.org.uk**

Macmillan **www.macmillan.org.uk/information-and-support/breast-cancer**

Cancer Research U.K **www.cancerresearchuk.org/about-cancer/breast-cancer**

Other books in this series

There are four books in total in this series which feature Lucy and Jack. Each Kidney book has two editions, one of which contains notes at the back for Parents and Professionals. Both editions are available from **Amazon.co.uk** and **Amazon.com**.

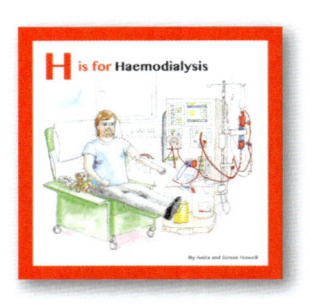

H is for Haemodialysis
Story Edition: http://amzn.eu/bzltqlG
Parent and Professional Edition: http://amzn.eu/d/gyKWkEj

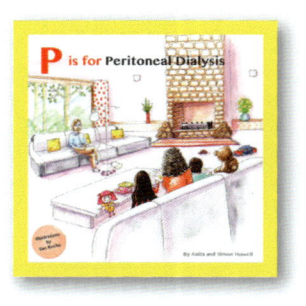

P is for Peritoneal Dialysis
Story Edition: http://amzn.eu/ahA40SL
Parent and Professional Edition: http://amzn.eu/d/2AUpllP

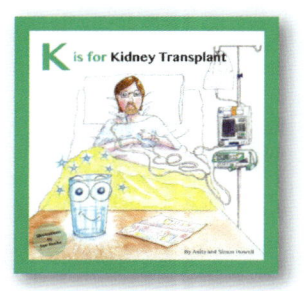

K is for Kidney Transplant
Story Edition: http://amzn.eu/3v72gys
Parent and Professional Edition: http://amzn.eu/d/gpEKEId

Printed in Great Britain
by Amazon